OLD MAN
DRINKS

OLD MAN DRINKS

RECIPES, ADVICE, AND BARSTOOL WISDOM

BY ROBERT SCHNAKENBERG

PHOTOS BY MICHAEL E. REALI

QUIRK BOOKS

PHILADELPHIA

Library of Congress Cataloging in Publication Number: 2009941370

ISBN: 978-1-59474-450-1
Printed in Singapore
Typeset in Akzidenz Grotesk, Bembo, and Trade Gothic

Edited by Sarah O'Brien
Designed by Doogie Horner
Photography by Michael E. Reali
Production management by John J. McGurk

10 9 8 7 6 5 4 3

Quirk Books
215 Church Street
Philadelphia, PA 19106
www.quirkbooks.com

TABLE OF CONTENTS

INTRODUCTION

S O YOU'VE MADE THE DECISION to start drinking like an old man. Congratulations on a great call! You're about to enter the final frontier of cocktail culture, a vast badlands where antique ingredients and fanciful names combine to create a drinking experience unlike any other—or at least unlike anything that anyone's experienced since at least the final months of the Eisenhower administration. In some cases, the recipes you'll find in this book date back to the nineteenth century—or even earlier. Call them *really* old man drinks. These are cocktails your great-grandfather would have remembered fondly from *his* early drinking days—a time of zoot suits and snap-brimmed hats and vendors selling pickles out of open barrels on the sidewalk. A time when a fella could saunter into his local tavern, slap his hand on the bar, and say, "Barkeep, fix me up a Sidecar!"—and not get himself laughed out of the room.

Fortunately, that time may be on its way back. Retro is in and everything old is new again—or at least new in the eyes of discriminating drinkers eager to take their style cues from 1960s advertising executives, hardboiled private eyes, Jazz-era night-club denizens, and other icons of our distant past. The one thing all these men had in common was a fondness for liquor—and lots of it. And we're talkin' the hard stuff: gin, Scotch, bourbon, and, of course, rye, the quintessential old-school whiskey whose very odor on the breath calls to mind your grandpa passed out on the couch at 2 A.M. on Christmas Eve. You won't find too many frou-frou girly drinks listed here. (Okay, you might find one or two, but even the hardest-drinking old man likes a change of pace every now and then.) Save your Woo Woos and your Cosmopolitans for the next meeting of the Ladies' Auxiliary. These are tough drinks, manly drinks, the kind the bartender has to check his cheat sheet to remember how to make. They take you back to another place and a distant time—and not just because of the high alcohol content. You can almost smell the wood paneling and cigar smoke as you inhale their names: the Whiskey Sour, the Boiler-maker, the Old Fashioned, and on and on.

To evoke the experience of drinking like an old man even more fully, we've included quotations from honest-to-goodness genuine old men, overheard in bar settings and reprinted with the permission of the ut-terer. In this way, you may drink in the observations of the old man you wish to emulate, even as you drink down the type of beverage that inspired his insight in the first place. As you make these drinks at home, or order them from a bewildered bartender, imagine yourself pulling up a stool next to some garrulous old-timer and engaging him in the most felicitous of conversations: one fueled by alcohol and good fellowship and brimming with intergenerational wisdom. At that moment, you will not merely be drinking like an old man. You will become one.

ALGONQUIN

Rye is the whiskey in this drink, which is named after the celebrated New York City hotel where literary luminaries once gathered. And wry was the type of wit dispensed around the hotel's fabled round table by Dorothy Parker, Robert Benchley, and their highfalutin' friends. But none of them ever drank an Algonquin *at* the Algonquin, because it was invented long after most of them had moved on to the Great Round Table in the sky. Too bad. This tart cocktail would have been right up Dorothy's alley.

Ingredients
2 ounces rye
1 ounce dry vermouth
1 ounce pineapple juice
Maraschino cherry

Preparation
Combine liquid ingredients in a cocktail shaker. Shake vigorously with ice. Strain into a cocktail glass. Garnish with a Maraschino cherry.

"No one said it better than Charles Baudelaire: 'Be drunk; be always drunk.' You can take that any way you like."

—Tom, 62, retired golf pro

ARNIE PALMER

Arnold Palmer was a helluva golfer—and an even better bartender. He knew that the best way to cool down after a rough back nine was with an ice-cold mix of iced tea and lemonade. Add a splash of vodka and you've got yourself the perfect remedy for a bad day on the links. Fore!

Ingredients
5 ounces iced tea
5 ounces lemonade
1 ounce vodka

Preparation
Combine ingredients in a tall glass filled with ice. Stir and enjoy.

AVIATION

This was one of the most popular cocktails of the 1930s, the era of "Lucky Lindy," Amelia Earhart, and the Hindenburg disaster. The stock market may have been crashing, but a couple glasses of this brew kept you in the clouds all night.

Ingredients
2 ounces gin
½ ounce Maraschino liqueur
½ ounce fresh lemon juice
Maraschino cherry

Preparation
Combine liquid ingredients in a cocktail shaker filled with ice. Shake well and then strain into a cocktail glass. Garnish with a Maraschino cherry.

"People would say, 'Oh, that's just one of the weirdos who drink out here.' Then I realized I *was* one of those weirdos."

—Anonymous

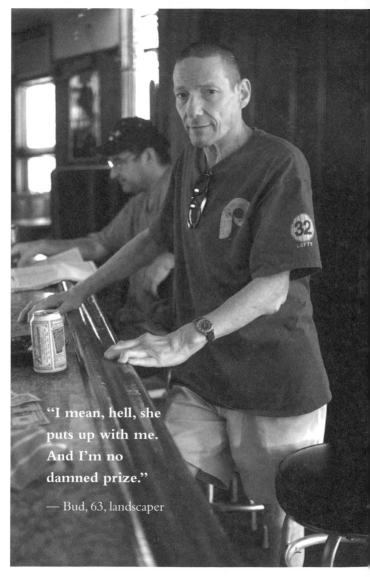

"I mean, hell, she puts up with me. And I'm no damned prize."

— Bud, 63, landscaper

BELLINI

Of all the great masterpieces to come out of the Italian Renaissance, this drink—named for the fifteenth-century Venetian painter Giovanni Bellini—may be the tastiest. (Try biting into a Titian some time and see what I mean.) Giuseppe Cipriani, the head bartender at Harry's Bar in Venice, is credited with inventing the Bellini sometime between 1934 and 1948. The pink color, he said, reminded him of a hue used by Bellini in one of his paintings. Drink a couple of these fizzy beauties and you'll be in the pink, too.

Ingredients
2 ounces peach puree (or peach nectar)
4 ounces chilled sparkling wine

Preparation
Pour the peach juice into a Champagne flute. Slowly add the sparkling wine. Stir and serve.

BLOODY MARY

There are almost as many suggested recipes as there are origin stories for this Sunday-brunch staple and traditional hangover cure, which may (or may not) have first been concocted by Fernand Petiot, a bartender at Harry's Bar in Paris, in the 1920s, or by entertainer George Jessel in the late 1930s. Add-ins may (or may not) include horseradish, olives, celery, beef bouillon, cayenne pepper, and various cold cuts used as garnish. One thing is (almost) certain: The gory cocktail was named after Mary Tudor, the queen of England. Or maybe it was Mary Pickford, the movie star. Or some woman in Chicago. Ahhh, forget it. Just make me one, stat, so I can get rid of this damned headache.

Ingredients
2 ounces vodka
6 ounces tomato juice
2 dashes Worcestershire sauce
Tabasco sauce (to taste)
Pinch of salt and pepper
½ ounce fresh lemon juice
Celery stalk

Preparation

Combine liquid ingredients and mix. Strain into a highball glass with ice. Garnish with a stalk of celery.

"Walking away is a woman's right. And then it's a man's right to watch her do it!"

—Andrew, 64, recruiter

BOILERMAKER

Back in the day, there used to be a thing called a shot and a beer. You drank your shot and then you chased it with a glass of beer. Then some genius came up with the idea of combining the two. Cut out the middleman. The guy who thought of this deserves a medal. Let's drink to him!

Ingredients
10 ounces beer
2 ounces whiskey

Preparation
Fill a shot glass with the whiskey of your choice. Drop the contents of the shot glass into a highball glass filled with beer. Drink immediately.

"Our music was so much better than now."

—Tom, 68, taxi driver

BRANDY ALEXANDER

If you don't like alcohol, this is the drink for you. This popular after-dinner cocktail has a creamy milkshake-like quality that all but masks the taste of the spirit. It dates back to 1922, when the bartender at London's Ciro Hotel created it to serve at the royal wedding of Princess Mary and Lord Alexander Lascelles in London. By the way, January 31 is National Brandy Alexander Day in the United States—whatever that means. You shouldn't let that stop you from drinking one year-round, preferably as the accompaniment to a good cigar.

Ingredients
1½ ounces brandy
1 ounce dark crème de cacao
1 ounce half-and-half
¼ teaspoon grated nutmeg

Preparation
In a shaker, combine the liquid ingredients and shake well. Strain into a cocktail glass and garnish with the grated nutmeg.

BRONX COCKTAIL

Otherwise known as a martini with orange juice, this cocktail was the Cosmopolitan of pre-Prohibition days. It was so wildly popular that President William Howard Taft caused a stir when he ordered one up with his AM meal. Opinions differ on who invented the Bronx (which was named after the Zoo, not the borough), with some evidence pointing to Waldorf-Astoria bartender Johnnie Solon and other sources crediting Joseph S. Sormani, a retired Bronx restaurant owner living in Philadelphia. Whoever came up with it, the drink was such a smash that at the height of its popularity, the Waldorf went through a case of oranges a day just to keep up with the demand.

Ingredients
2 ounces gin
½ ounce dry vermouth
½ ounce sweet vermouth
1 ounce fresh orange juice
Orange slice

Preparation
Shake liquid ingredients well with ice and strain into a cocktail glass. Garnish with an orange slice.

"You have Champagne tastes and beer pockets."

—Merle, 73, engineer

CHAMPAGNE COCKTAIL

The year 1934 was a good one for Clark Gable, FDR, and the Champagne cocktail—which was designated by *Esquire* magazine as one of the year's top ten cocktails. A decidedly luxe drink beloved by wealthy swells the world over, it actually dates back to the Gilded Age, when a shiny top hat and a monocle were all a fella needed to get by. Try one at your next New Year's Eve bash, Oscar night party, or yacht christening. If the man on the Monopoly box had a favorite drink, this would be it.

Ingredients
1 sugar cube
2 to 3 dashes Angostura bitters
1 ounce brandy
6 ounces chilled Champagne
Lemon twist

Preparation
Soak the sugar cube in the Angostura bitters and place it in the bottom of a Champagne flute. Add the brandy. Fill the glass with Champagne. Garnish with a twist of lemon.

CLOVER CLUB

Named for a high-class Philadelphia men's club where the captains of industry gathered in pre-Prohibition days, the Clover Club was once the quintessential gentleman's cocktail. Mixologist Jack Townsend, author of the 1951 classic *The Bartender's Book*, referred to the typical Clover Club drinker as "the distinguished patron of the oak-paneled lounge." Sad to say, the drink has declined in popularity. Maybe it's the presence of the raw egg white, which could put even the hardiest mogul off his feed. Decide for yourself—and worry about the salmonella later.

Ingredients
1½ ounces gin
¾ ounce lemon juice
¼ ounce grenadine
1 egg white

Preparation
Combine all ingredients and shake vigorously. Strain into a cocktail glass.

"I don't care. You inflicted the pain, you still got to get up and work."

—Daniel, 62, auto body repairman (about hard drinking after work)

"Real old-school stuff, you see. That's why they had those brass rails running across the top of the bar. You stayed on your feet. Once you began to lean over the bar, that's how the barkeep knew you were done, and he'd kick you."

—Neil, 67, laborer

CUBA LIBRE

Return to those glorious pre-Castro days when gangsters ruled Cuba and Coca-Cola flowed freely in the Mafia-owned casinos. This refreshing cocktail was first concocted in 1900, the year U.S. soldiers introduced soda pop to the island. It later inspired a hit song by the Andrews Sisters titled, appropriately enough, "Rum and Coca-Cola." The proper toast when drinking it is: "To a free and independent Cuba!"

Ingredients
Juice of half a lime
2 ounces light rum
Coca-Cola
Lime wedge

Preparation
Pour the lime juice into a highball glass filled with ice. Add the rum and then fill with the cola. Stir. Garnish with a wedge of lime and serve.

"That's all I did on my down time. Sit around and get shitfaced. All the time. Then I'd go and work for a week or so. Then get shitfaced again. What can I say, I get bored easily. It helped kill time."

— Patrick, 65, trucker

"People don't understand respect anymore.
Used to be, if a guy was stand-up, you
could trust his word. Not like now.
'Course you never wanted to cross these
guys either. You'd pay, no matter how slick
you thought you were."

—Jeff, 65, retired store owner

DEMPSEY COCKTAIL

Jack Dempsey, heavyweight champion from 1919 to 1926, packed quite a punch. His namesake cocktail? Not so much. Maybe "The Manassa Mauler," as he was called, mellowed as he got older. That could explain the presence of so many genteel ingredients in this drink, which won't knock you out so much as lull you into submission. Could be it was designed for the more re-fined palates of the wealthy swells who packed the ring-side seats at Dempsey's fights.

Ingredients
1 ounce apple brandy
1 ounce gin
1 teaspoon anise liqueur
½ teaspoon grenadine

Preparation
Stir all ingredients with ice, strain into a cocktail glass, and serve.

DRY MAHONEY

Bored with the same old gin and vodka martinis? Swap in some Kentucky whiskey and you've got yourself a Dry Mahoney, the perfect capper to a day spent overseeing your plantation. Relax in the wood-paneled splendor of your local gentleman's club and drift away . . .

Ingredients
2½ ounces bourbon
½ ounce dry vermouth
Lemon twist

Preparation
Combine liquid ingredients in a shaker with ice. Strain into a chilled cocktail glass. Garnish with the lemon twist and serve.

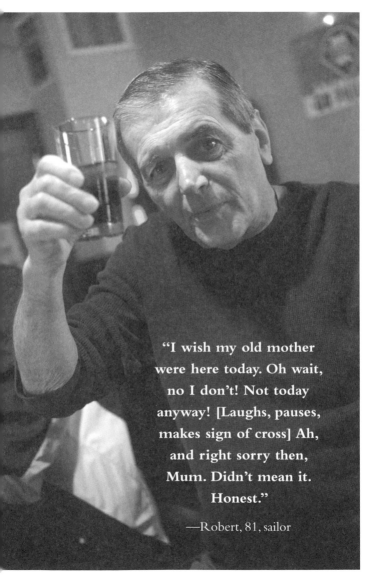

"I wish my old mother were here today. Oh wait, no I don't! Not today anyway! [Laughs, pauses, makes sign of cross] Ah, and right sorry then, Mum. Didn't mean it. Honest."

—Robert, 81, sailor

"My ladies were all classy.
Dressed well."

—Bill, 65, butcher

DUBONNET COCKTAIL

Queen Elizabeth is one classy dame, so when she puts her stamp of approval on a drink, that's good enough for me. Her Majesty's a big fan of the Dubonnet Cocktail, a Prohibition favorite that actually dates back to the mid-nineteenth century. Dubonnet is a wine-based aperitif flavored with quinine that was originally imbibed by French Foreign Legionnaires in North Africa in order to stave off malaria. A nice dose will cure that and whatever else ails you. Substitute red vermouth for the gin, and you've got yourself a Lady Madonna.

Ingredients
1½ ounces gin
1½ ounces red Dubonnet
Dash of bitters
Lemon twist

Preparation
Shake the liquid ingredients with ice and strain into a chilled cocktail glass. Garnish with the lemon twist.

EL PRESIDENTE

The "presidente" in this case would be Gerardo Machado, the right-wing strongman who ruled Cuba with an iron fist from 1925 to 1933. This particular drink was first concocted by an American bartender working at the Jockey Club in Havana during Prohibition. According to legend, Machado once offered one to Calvin Coolidge while the U.S. president was attending a conference in Havana. "Silent Cal" declined. The easy-sipping drink later became the house cocktail at the swank Club El Chico in Manhattan's Greenwich Village, where the high-hatted swells dubbed it "an elixir for jaded gullets."

Ingredients
1½ ounces white rum
¾ ounce orange curaçao
¾ ounce dry vermouth
Dash of grenadine

Preparation
Pour all ingredients into a cocktail shaker with ice. Shake vigorously and then strain into a cocktail glass.

"Always try to achieve your goals. But that's not for everyone."

—Clifford, 60, musician

FINE AND DANDY

Everything will seem that way after you've pounded back a couple of these lovelies. The name evokes a style, an attitude, and a mode of living associated with the well-heeled fops of a bygone era. The golden age of dandyism may have been the first half of the nineteenth century, which is when Thomas Carlyle defined the dandy as "a clothes-wearing man, a man whose trade, office, and existence consists in the wearing of clothes." Today we know them as *metrosexuals*, although *macaroni* and *popinjay* are all acceptable synonyms. This is a stylish drink for a stylish man of any age—though the older you are, the more likely you can get away with wearing lace-cuffed shirts and velvet smoking jackets.

Ingredients
2 ounces gin
1 ounce Triple Sec
1 ounce lemon juice
Dash of orange bitters

Preparation
Combine all ingredients and shake well with ice. Strain into a cocktail glass.

GIBSON

They do a lot of strange things in San Francisco. One odd practice is putting onions in their martinis, which they've been doing since the late nineteenth century. Named after the man who first ordered it—Bay Area barfly Walter D. K. Gibson (who believed that eating onions would fend off colds)—this halitosis-inducing cocktail has long been erroneously associated with the great *Life* magazine illustrator Charles Dana Gibson, who had nothing to do with its invention (and no theories about onions to speak of).

Ingredients
¾ ounce chilled dry vermouth
2 ounces chilled gin
1 small pearl cocktail onion

Preparation
Pour the liquid ingredients into a cocktail shaker with ice. Shake well and strain into a cocktail glass. Garnish with a skewered cocktail onion.

"I can drink whatever I like tonight as long as tomorrow I eat chicken soup."

—Ari, 71, lawyer

GIMLET

━━━━━━━━━━━
━━━━━━━━━━━

"A real gimlet is half gin and half Rose's Lime Juice and nothing else," declares dissolute playboy Terry Lennox in Raymond Chandler's novel *The Long Goodbye*. "It beats martinis hollow." I'm inclined to agree with that last part—and though the one-to-one ratio might be a little sweet for some tastes, the simple elegance of the traditional gimlet recipe can't be topped. Like Chandler's prose, it's spare but packs a wallop. Gimlets first became popular in the 1920s, before Philip Marlowe was even old enough to order one. The wizened private dick drank plenty of them over the course of twenty years and seven novels—and not one of them contained vodka or (God forbid) tequila. But it's the citrus that really makes the drink. As Marlowe himself observed: "The bartender set the drink in front of me. With the lime juice it has a sort of pale greenish yellowish misty look. I tasted it. It was both sweet and sharp at the same time." Damn straight.

Ingredients

2 ounces gin
1 ounce Rose's Lime Juice
Lime wedge

Preparation

Mix the liquid ingredients in a cocktail shaker with ice. Shake well. Strain into a chilled cocktail glass. Garnish with the lime wedge.

"They can bring it up faster than you can drink it."

—Dick, 80, factory worker

GIN AND MILK

God bless the mad genius who decided to mix these two ingredients. If nothing else, the gin will kill any germs, so it's a great way to polish off leftover milk that's reached the end of its lifespan. Plus, if you're a lush, you can pound these down all day long in front of clients, kids—even your AA sponsor—and no one's the wiser. Promotes healthy bones and teeth, too. Yessir, gin and milk's got a *whole* lot going for it.

Ingredients
2 ounces gin
1 cup milk
Nutmeg

Preparation
Combine the liquid ingredients and shake with ice. Strain into a Collins glass. Sprinkle with nutmeg and serve.

"The definition of an alcoholic? Someone who goes into a bar with an 'All You Can Drink for $1' sign and says, 'Give me two dollars' worth, please.'"

—Anonymous

GIN AND TONIC

What could be better than drinking for "medicinal" purposes? This classic warm-weather cocktail was originally concocted by British troops in Asia as a means of staving off malaria, though the hard truth is you'd have to consume something like seventeen gallons of the stuff in a twenty-four-hour period to deliver the requisite dose of quinine and achieve the preventative benefits (which, on a hot July day, is not impossible, provided you live near a lime orchard).

Ingredients
2 ounces gin
5 ounces tonic water
Lime wedge

Preparation
Pour the gin and tonic water into a highball glass nearly filled with ice cubes. Stir well. Garnish with the lime wedge.

GIN RICKEY

Credit the oppressive heat of a Washington, D.C., summer
for this one. Back in the days before air conditioning,
drunkards in America's capital needed refreshing cocktails
to cool them down. One such barfly was Colonel Joe
Rickey, a Congressional lobbyist who wandered into a watering hole called Shoemaker's in the middle of a heat
wave and drank the first thing the bartender set down in
front of him. The lime juice and gin libation so quenched
his thirst that the mixologist immediately christened the
drink the Gin Rickey, in his honor. It's been greasing the
gears of government officials ever since.

Ingredients
2 ounces gin
Juice of one lime
Club soda
Lime wedge

Preparation
Fill a highball glass with ice. Pour in the gin and lime
juice. Top with the club soda and garnish with a lime
wedge.

"Remember [Massachusetts] Governor Bill Weld? If you could go out drinking until late and still make it to work the next day, you were okay in his book. Same with me."

—Leo, 75, retired banker

GIN SOUR

Popular in the 1940s, gin sours went out of fashion along with the Edsel, the poodle skirt, and the Truman administration. But just like Give 'Em Hell Harry, this one is primed for a comeback. For authentic Prohibition-era flavor, use bathtub gin instead of that fancy bottled stuff.

Ingredients

2 ounces gin
1 ounce lemon juice
½ teaspoon superfine sugar
Cherry

Preparation

Shake first three ingredients in a shaker with ice. Strain into a sour glass. Garnish with a cherry.

GRASSHOPPER

If you enjoy after-dinner mints, then this is the drink for you. A creamy green concoction first whipped up at Tujague's bar in the French Quarter of New Orleans, it took the American South by storm in the 1950s and '60s and is one of two cocktails most associated with the Big Easy. The Hurricane is the other.

Ingredients
¾ ounce green crème de menthe
¾ ounce white crème de cacao
¾ ounce light cream

Preparation
Shake all ingredients with ice. Strain into a cocktail glass and serve.

"You work hard, you have a roof over your head and food in your belly. To me, that was success. Nowadays, people ain't happy without their toys."

—Peter, 70, accountant

"Drinking was just one of those things we did. Almost everyone drank. It was a common thing."

—Henry, 65, carpenter

GRUMPY OLD MAN

This drink is *so* old man it's got "old man" in the name. Most recipes suggest you ratchet up the decrepitude even further by using Old Grand-Dad high-proof bourbon. Swap in some sour mix for the ginger ale, and you've got yourself a Grumpier Old Man. Come to think of it, that much sour mix would make a young man grumpy, too.

Ingredients
2 ounces bourbon
1 ounce lime juice
Ginger ale

Preparation
Pour the bourbon into an Old Fashioned glass filled with ice. Add the lime juice and top with the ginger ale. Serve.

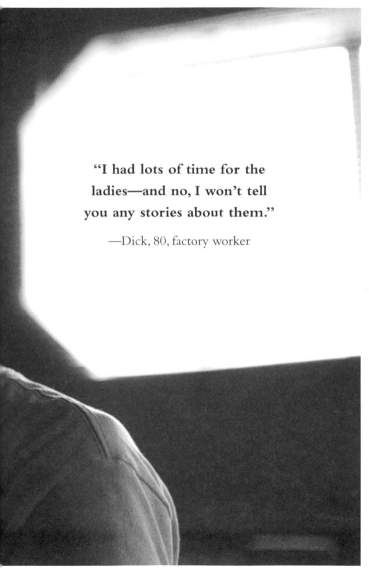

"I had lots of time for the ladies—and no, I won't tell you any stories about them."

—Dick, 80, factory worker

HARVEY WALLBANGER

Sometimes the name really makes the drink. Consider the Harvey Wallbanger. It's basically a screwdriver with a dash of Galliano added in, but thanks mostly to its distinctive, vaguely smutty-sounding moniker (and a promotional ad campaign featuring a lovable cartoon character by that name) it became one of the most popular cocktails of the 1970s. Legend has it the Harvey was created in the 1950s by Donato "Duke" Antone, the famed Los Angeles mixologist who also gave the world the Rusty Nail, the Flaming Caesar, and the Godfather. The name was inspired by a drunken patron who kept banging into walls one day after downing one too many. Order one up the next time you're "flying high" (the Wallbanger became a worldwide sensation after TWA began serving it in its 747 cocktail lounges) or dispense as an accompaniment to a menu of old-school entrée favorites, like Veal Prince Orloff or Boeuf Bourguignon. This is powerful stuff, so don't be surprised if you're banging into a few walls yourself by the end of the evening.

Ingredients

1 ounce vodka
4 ounces orange juice
½ ounce Galliano

Preparation

Pour vodka and orange juice into a Collins glass over
ice cubes and stir. Float the Galliano on top and serve.

**"I've seen it, kid. When the man
is no longer in charge, and the
drink takes over."**

—Arnie, 75, "businessman"

"The older I get, the less I talk."

—Wes, 62, construction worker

HIGHBALL

Highball, in this case, is the name of the drink, not the class of drinks customarily served in a tall (highball) glass. Got that? Try keeping it straight after pounding away a couple of these. Just to confuse things further, there are many different varieties of Highball—including ones made with gin (known as a Bulldog Highball), bourbon, bitters, and Irish whiskey. Choose your favorite or stick with this basic recipe, which uses that classic old man spirit, rye.

Ingredients
2 ounces rye
Ginger ale

Preparation
Fill a highball glass with ice. Pour in the rye. Top with the ginger ale.

HOT TODDY

A piping hot mug of this stuff will cure what ails you. In fact, the hot toddy has long been considered a cracker-jack cold and flu remedy—despite the American Medical Association's recommendations to the contrary. But hey, what do those doctors know? I know that when I drink this on a cold winter's night, I feel better immediately. Besides, if alcohol didn't have some health benefit, they wouldn't put it in cough medicine, right? Feel free to swap in your preferred whiskey for the rum. Cloves, ground cinnamon, and nutmeg are all traditional add-ins as well. Oh, and the name *toddy* apparently derives from the sap of an Asian palm tree. But that's a whole other story. . . .

Ingredients
1 ounce rum
1 ounce honey
1 ounce lemon juice
Boiling water
Cinnamon stick

Preparation

Combine the first three ingredients in a mug. Pour in enough boiling water to fill and stir with a cinnamon stick. Allow to cool slightly before serving.

"That guy Spock was an idiot. My kids turned out okay because my wife and me raised 'em like we were raised."

—Ron, 72, retired teacher

HURRICANE

Ordinarily we wouldn't endorse any alcoholic beverage served in a plastic cup, but we'll make an exception in the case of this easy-sipping New Orleans classic, which was first whipped up by a bartender at Pat O'Brien's Bar in the French Quarter sometime in the 1940s. Truth be told, you'd have to be a pretty fey old man to drink this in public, but in the spirit of *laissez les bons temps rouler*—and because it's so damn hot down there—we'll allow it. Besides, if the people of the Big Easy can survive a real hurricane, they've earned the chance to drink whatever they like. Two of these on a July day and you'll be flying into the eye under your own power.

Ingredients

2 ounces light rum
2 ounces dark rum
2 ounces passion fruit juice
1 ounce orange juice
½ ounce fresh lime juice
1 tablespoon simple syrup*
1 tablespoon grenadine
Maraschino cherry
Orange slice

Preparation

Shake liquid ingredients vigorously with ice and strain into a hurricane glass. Garnish with a cherry and an orange slice.

---

* To prepare simple syrup, combine one cup of sugar with one cup of water in a saucepan and bring to a boil. Stir until sugar dissolves. Cool.

"You cannot dedicate your life to drinking. You've got to know how to deal with sober people."

—Ceasar, 60, engineer and painter

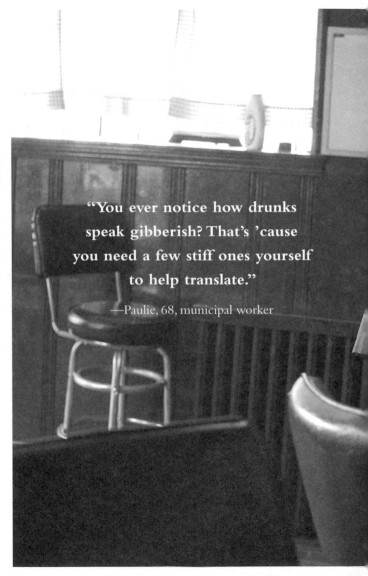

"You ever notice how drunks speak gibberish? That's 'cause you need a few stiff ones yourself to help translate."

—Paulie, 68, municipal worker

IRISH COFFEE

It was a cold winter's eve in 1942, and a group of American airline passengers found themselves stranded at Foyne's Airbase in Limerick, Ireland, due to bad weather. (Is there any other kind in Ireland?) Enter Joe Sheridan, a chef in a restaurant in the terminal building, who invented this ingenious libation on the spot as a means of comforting the tired and cranky travelers. When one guest asked Sheridan if he was serving them Brazilian coffee, the chef replied, "No, that's Irish coffee." And another chapter in Ireland's rich history of drink was written.

Ingredients
1 cup hot brewed coffee
Sugar, to taste
1 ounce Irish whiskey
1 tablespoon whipped cream

Preparation
Fill a mug with hot coffee and add as much sugar as you desire. Add the whiskey and top with a dab of whipped cream.

"Can you help me write a text message to my wife? She's very upset with me and I don't deal well with cell phones."

—Gary, 68, retired bus driver

JACK COLLINS

Tom may get all the attention in the Collins family, but his little brother Jack packs quite a wallop himself. (And don't even get us started on their no-good sister Brandy or their cousins John, Mike, Pedro, Sandy, and Vodka.) The presence of applejack is what really pushes this one into Old Man territory. You can easily imagine Washington Irving's Rip Van Winkle brewing up the basic ingredient for this drink in a makeshift still behind his clapboard house.

Ingredients
1½ ounces applejack
1 ounce lemon juice
1 teaspoon simple syrup (see recipe on page 65)
Dash orange bitters
Club soda
Lemon slice

Preparation
Combine the first four ingredients with ice and shake. Pour into a chilled Collins glass. Fill with club soda and stir. Garnish with a lemon slice.

JACK ROSE

Some people work *way* too hard trying to understand the name behind a drink. Take the Jack Rose, for example. Over the decades—and it has been decades since anybody drank one of these—imaginative tipplers have suggested it was named after everyone from Bald Jack Rose—a World War I–era gangland figure—to a New Jersey bartender. But the Jack in this case refers to applejack, the base spirit, and the Rose indicates the cocktail's overall pinkish hue. The other noteworthy thing about this drink is that it's mentioned in *The Sun Also Rises*, meaning that Papa Hemingway himself must have tried one at some point. And that's a literary stamp of approval every old man would want on his cocktail.

Ingredients
½ ounce fresh lemon juice
1½ ounces applejack
1 teaspoon grenadine

Preparation
Combine all ingredients with cracked ice and shake. Strain into a chilled cocktail glass.

KIR ROYALE

Life in Nazi-occupied France was no picnic. (Unless you were a German soldier, of course, then it was pretty much a picnic all the time.) When they weren't thinking up new ways to surrender, the French turned to the leaders of the Resistance for inspiration. One such leader was Canon Félix Kir, the mayor of Dijon and a stalwart French patriot. A sort of junior varsity Oskar Schindler, Kir helped about five thousand of his compatriots to escape from the Nazis. But his greatest contribution to history may have been his favorite cocktail, a sweet, fizzy combination of Chardonnay and crème de cassis that came to be known as the Kir, in his honor. Class it up with Champagne instead of still wine and you've got what's known as a Kir Royale, which today is the preferred version of the drink. Mix one up on New Year's Eve, Bastille Day, or anytime you want to celebrate the splendor that is France—and get rid of that ancient bottle of crème de cassis that's been gathering dust in the back of your liquor cabinet. *Vive la résistance!*

Ingredients

5 ounces chilled Champagne
1 ounce crème de cassis
Lemon twist

Preparation

Pour the Champagne into a Champagne flute. Add the crème de cassis. Garnish with a lemon twist.

"You know, women are both
wonderful and major trouble.
I love it!"

—Al, 65, department manager

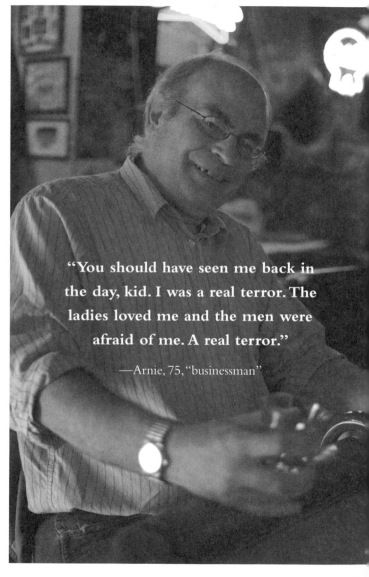

"You should have seen me back in the day, kid. I was a real terror. The ladies loved me and the men were afraid of me. A real terror."

—Arnie, 75, "businessman"

MANHATTAN

Take a trip back to the Gilded Age with this classic cocktail, which was reportedly invented in 1874 at New York's Manhattan Club at a reception in honor of Governor William Tilden. Winston Churchill's mother was one of the first people to drink one, and it was the cocktail of choice for Frank Sinatra and his Rat Pack, so you know it's as old school as it gets. For a more authentic nineteenth-century experience, substitute rye for the bourbon. That's the way Diamond Jim Brady would have made it.

Ingredients
2 ounces bourbon
1 ounce sweet vermouth
Dash Angostura bitters
Maraschino cherry

Preparation
Combine the liquid ingredients in cocktail shaker filled with ice. Shake vigorously and strain into a cocktail glass. Garnish with a Maraschino cherry.

MARTINEZ

And the Manhattan begat the Martinez, which begat the Martini, and all was well in the Kingdom of Vermouth. The humble Martinez tends to get lost in the shuffle between these two giants of cocktaildom, but it's quite an elegant drink in its own right. First concocted at the height of the California Gold Rush to placate a forty-niner who had wandered into the town of Martinez and wanted to celebrate his gold strike, it's rarely served today—but it's due for a hipster-led revival. Early recipes called for a wine glass full of vermouth, which may explain why so many gold prospectors wound up prematurely grizzled.

Ingredients
2 ounces gin
1 ounce sweet vermouth
¼ ounce Maraschino liqueur
Dash orange bitters

Preparation
Combine all ingredients in a shaker and shake. Strain into a chilled cocktail glass.

MARTINI

What can one say about the King of Cocktails that hasn't already been said? It is descended from the Manhattan by way of the Martinez, though its distinctive moniker may derive from Martini di Arma di Taggia, the head bartender at New York City's Knickerbocker Hotel, who may (or may not) have invented the drink there in 1911. (Legend has it that oil magnate John D. Rockefeller was the first to try one.) The search for the truth about the martini's origins is almost as vexing as the quest to come up with the perfect method of making one. Everyone has an opinion about the proper ratio of vermouth to gin and how vigorously the contents should be agitated. James Bond, of course, liked his martinis "shaken, not stirred," but W. Somerset Maugham preferred the latter action "so that the molecules lie sensuously one on top of the other." Other famous historical martini drinkers include Humphrey Bogart, George Burns, F. Scott Fitzgerald, Dean Martin, Franklin Delano Roosevelt, and esteemed literary critic Bernard DeVoto, who called the drink "the supreme American gift to world culture." Blend according to your own taste. You can even make it with vodka—if you must—but on no account should any self-respecting old man give in to the modern mania for attaching the suffix "-tini" to every Tom, Dick, and Harry drink that comes down the pike. That's just plain wrong.

Ingredients
2½ ounces gin
½ ounce dry vermouth
Green olive

Preparation
Combine the gin and vermouth, stir, and strain into a chilled cocktail glass. Garnish with a green olive.

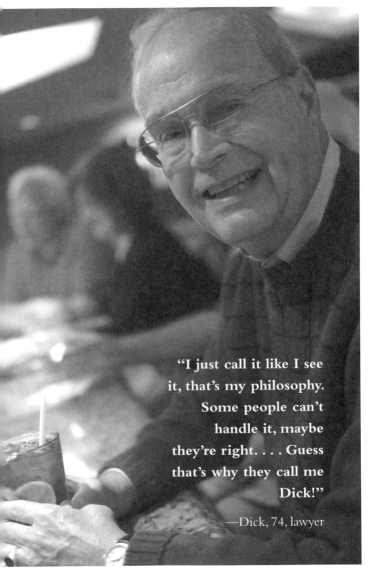

"I just call it like I see it, that's my philosophy. Some people can't handle it, maybe they're right. . . . Guess that's why they call me Dick!"

—Dick, 74, lawyer

"I can't believe I just threw you down the stairs in front of my grandson's guidance counselor."

—Jim, 69, retired chef

MARY PICKFORD

That Mary Pickford sure had nice gams. In the 1920s, about the only thing that could take a man's mind off those stems was this cocktail, which was named for the silent movie star by a bartender in Havana. It's sweet and tart—just like "America's Sweetheart" herself.

Ingredients
2 ounces light rum
2 ounces pineapple juice
1 teaspoon grenadine
1 teaspoon Maraschino liqueur
Lime twist

Preparation
Pour the liquid ingredients into a cocktail shaker with ice cubes. Shake well and then strain into a cocktail glass. Garnish with a lime twist.

MATADOR

Forget the Margarita. To heck with the Tequila Sunrise. This drink may have done more for the Mexican economy than those two cocktails put together. The Matador uses three of Mexico's most exported foodstuffs: pineapple, lime, and tequila. The perfect old man thirst quencher, it adapts well to lazy afternoons on the shuffleboard court in Boca or the clubhouse after a rough back nine on a hot day. And because it's sweeter and fruitier than the Margarita, it's a great drink to share with the old lady in your life. Send one over to that sexy widow from the adjacent condo you've had your eye on. Pretty soon the two of you will be making beautiful mariachi music together.

Ingredients
3 ounces pineapple juice
1½ ounces tequila
Juice of one lime

Preparation
Combine all ingredients in a shaker with ice and shake. Strain into a Champagne flute and serve.

"Tacos make me very angry."

—Paul, 65, museum curator

MINT JULEP

"A whiskey julep," wrote poet John Reuben Thompson, "is the drink that typifies the nation." By "nation" he meant his native Virginia, and by extension the rest of what would become known as the Confederate States of America. The drink of choice among old Southern crackers for generations, the Mint Julep is another one of those cocktails—like the Martini—that inspires a lot of debate. Julep aficionados argue most heatedly over whether you should crush, or muddle, the fresh mint to release its essential oils. Do what you think is necessary—just don't make one with anything besides top-quality Kentucky bourbon. Anything else is an insult to your Dixie forebears. The other bone of contention concerns the drink's origin. The julep's backstory is murkier and more drenched in Southern Gothic mythology than a Faulkner novel. Two things we know for certain: 1) The word *julep*, meaning "rose water," derives from Arabic; and 2) this drink has been served annually at the Kentucky Derby since 1875. No matter which side of the Civil War your ancestors fought on, we can all agree: After a bad day at the track, slamming back a couple of these is the perfect way to drown your sorrows.

Ingredients

1 tablespoon simple syrup (see recipe on page 65)
5 or 6 sprigs fresh mint
4 ounces bourbon

Preparation

Add the syrup and mint to a glass filled with crushed ice. Fill the glass with bourbon and serve.

"Here's to you and yours, and to mine and ours, and if you and yours ever comes across cross mine and ours, then may you and yours do the . . . wait, or is it the . . . ah, to hell with it. I could never remember any of that damn stuff anyway. Best to be original, right?"

—Peter, 77, floor manager

MONKEY GLAND

They say that W. B. Yeats had monkey glands implanted in his scrotum when he was an old man, to help restore his sexual potency. That revolutionary procedure, which was all the rage in the 1920s, provided the inspiration for this cocktail, first mixed up by Harry MacElhone, owner of Harry's New York Bar in Paris. The *Washington Post* pronounced it the smash hit of the 1923 French tourist season, and it was later adjudged to be one of the quintessential cocktails of the Prohibition era. No representations are made or implied regarding this drink's—*ahem*—rejuvenating—powers, though it is a fact that Yeats got his groove back soon after undergoing the procedure.

Ingredients
2 ounces gin
1 ounce orange juice
Dash grenadine
Dash absinthe

Preparation
Combine all ingredients and shake well. Strain into a cocktail glass and serve.

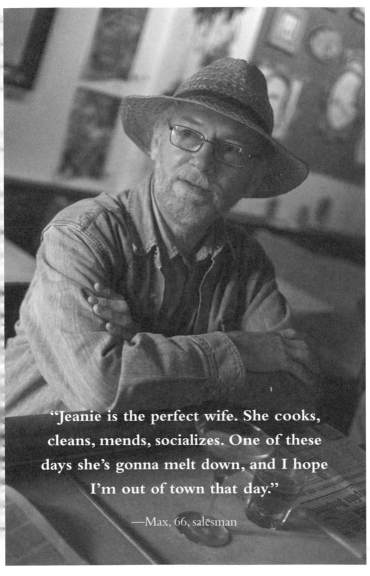

"Jeanie is the perfect wife. She cooks, cleans, mends, socializes. One of these days she's gonna melt down, and I hope I'm out of town that day."

—Max, 66, salesman

"I don't think I've got a gambling addiction. I do have a life addiction, and life's a gamble!"

—Pete, 68, undisclosed

MONTE CARLO

After a long evening at the baccarat table, there's no better way to unwind and forget about your losses than with a nice stiff whiskey drink named after the famed resort city of Monaco. Benedictine is a sweet liqueur named for the Benedictine monks who first produced it back in the sixteenth century. If you can't find it, you could always try making a Monte Carlo Imperial instead—a totally different drink consisting of gin, crème de menthe, lemon juice, and Champagne that is sometimes referred to simply as a Monte Carlo. Both are perfectly delicious old man drinks that will have you staggering back to the gaming tables in no time.

Ingredients
2 ounces rye
¾ ounce Benedictine
2 dashes Peychaud's bitters
Maraschino cherry

Preparation
Combine liquid ingredients and shake vigorously with ice. Strain into a cocktail glass. Garnish with a Maraschino cherry.

"Ain't like it used to be. Back then, a lot of these bars were dark little places, holes in the wall, you see. People didn't go there to be social; they went there to get potted drunk. Not like now; now, they look like a McDonalds."

—Mike, 62, custodian

NEGRONI

That would be Count Camillo Negroni, the debauched Florentine nobleman who supposedly invented this classic Italian aperitif as a hangover cure in the dark days following World War I. Think of it as a bitter, medicinal-tasting Martini and you'll have some idea of the lip-puckering tartness that awaits you when you mix up one of these babies. Supposedly it stimulates the appetite and focuses the mind, although depending on your taste for cough syrup it may only stimulate you to order something else next time. But if you're down for the Count, try making yours a double.

Ingredients
1 ounce gin
1 ounce Campari
¾ ounce sweet vermouth
Orange twist

Preparation
Combine liquid ingredients and ice and shake well. Strain into a chilled cocktail glass. Garnish with an orange twist.

"I know it sounds stupid, but I can't handle being sober in a room full of drunks. Drinking with them—now, that's a different story."

—Fred, 68, writer

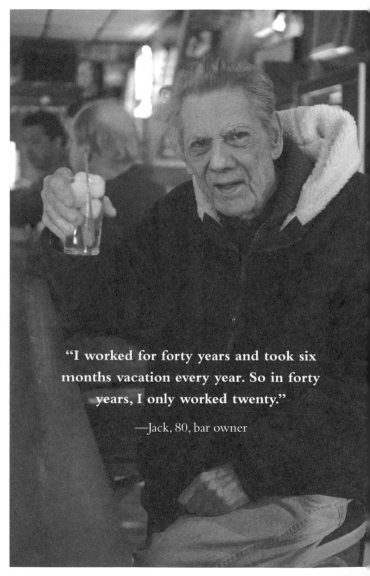

"I worked for forty years and took six months vacation every year. So in forty years, I only worked twenty."

—Jack, 80, bar owner

NEW YORK COCKTAIL

Not to be confused with a Manhattan, this sweet cocktail provides ersatz Big Apple flavor for old men who wouldn't be caught dead in any of the Five Boroughs. Use premium Canadian whiskey for the best effect.

Ingredients
2 ounces blended whiskey
1 ounce lemon juice
½ teaspoon grenadine
1 teaspoon superfine sugar
Lemon twist

Preparation
Combine liquid ingredients and sugar, shake well with ice, and strain into a chilled cocktail glass. Garnish with a lemon twist.

NIGHT CAP

Used to be when someone invited you up for a night cap, you knew you were about to get lucky. Then you became an old man, and the person inviting you to drink one was your wife or, quite possibly, your nurse. At that point, a night cap became a warm coffee-flavored concoction designed to make you fall asleep as quickly as possible. Drink this if you want to fall asleep as quickly as possible. Waking up again—well, that's up to you.

Ingredients
1 ounce Kahlua
1 teaspoon powdered sugar
6 ounces warm milk
Dash nutmeg

Preparation
Pour Kahlua and sugar into a mug. Fill with warm milk and sprinkle nutmeg on top.

OBITUARY

Old men spend a lot of time reading the obituaries. So why not drink a few while you scour the agate for the names of your old friends? This cocktail turns the Martini on its head with the addition of absinthe, which, if you were taking an extended whiz in 2007 and didn't hear the news, is now legal again in the United States. Back in the day, people claimed that absinthe could cure malaria, give you seizures, and make you see things that weren't there. All it ever did for me was turn my drinks green and make everything taste like licorice.

Ingredients
2 ounces gin
¼ ounce dry vermouth
¼ ounce absinthe

Preparation
Combine all ingredients with cracked ice and stir well. Strain into a chilled cocktail glass.

"If I had a nickel for every pretty girl I bought a drink, well, I'd still be far behind."

—Neil, 67, laborer

OLD FASHIONED

This may be the quintessential Old Man Drink. It's so old, it was being called "old-fashioned" in the *1890s*. It's so old, one of the glasses we drink cocktails out of is *named* after it. It's so old, some scholars believe it was the first drink to be *called* a cocktail. A potent combination of whiskey, sugar, and bitters that's served on the rocks, the O. F. shouldn't be muddied up with a lot of unnecessary fruit, as some mixologists do. (It should, however, be *muddled* up, as in agitated with a muddler, so invest in a good one if you want to add this to your menu.) A simple garnish of lemon peel is all you need to add the perfect aromatic note to this sweet-and-sour classic.

Ingredients
1 sugar cube
2 dashes Angostura bitters
2 ounces bourbon
Lemon twist

Preparation
Muddle the sugar cube and bitters in the bottom of an Old Fashioned glass. Add ice and bourbon. Stir. Garnish with a lemon twist.

"A woman has different personalities;
they change every day."

—Stu, 64, lawyer

"How do we get along so well? Easy. I lie to her and she lies to me. It's understood. We don't really want to know."

—Al, 65, department manager

OLD PAL

Who doesn't need a helping hand from an Old Pal every now and then? Like the friend you never talk to but who is always available to help you move, this easy-sipping variation on the Martini is at your service 24/7, asking little in return. Dating back to the turn of the twentieth century, it's one of the first recorded recipes to call for Campari as an ingredient.

Ingredients

1 ounce rye
¾ ounce dry vermouth
¾ ounce Campari
Lemon twist

Preparation

Combine liquid ingredients with ice and stir. Strain into a cocktail glass. Garnish with a lemon twist.

PADDY COCKTAIL

Also known as an Irish Manhattan, this drink has a politically incorrect name but a more authentic heritage than such kitschy St. Patrick's Day cocktails as the O'Jito and the Emerald. In this case, the "Paddy" element is added by substituting Irish whiskey for bourbon. Otherwise, the proportions are exactly the same as the Manhattan. It's one in a class of ethnically insensitive riffs on classic drinks that includes the Paisley Martini and the Bobby Burns.

Ingredients
1 ounce Irish whiskey
1 ounce sweet vermouth
Dash Angostura bitters
Lemon twist

Preparation
Shake liquid ingredients with ice and strain into a cocktail glass. Garnish with a twist of lemon.

"I drank so much, I was sober.
Then I had a few more."

—Leo, 88, retired military

PIMM'S CUP

Tennis, anyone? What the Mint Julep is to the Kentucky Derby, this drink is to the annual championships held at the All-England Tennis Club, otherwise known as Wimbledon. Created in 1840 by London bartender James Pimm, Pimm's Cup has been a warm-weather favorite for Britons ever since. The proprietary gin-based spirit isn't widely available outside the United Kingdom, and the secret recipe is said to be known by only six people at any one time, but you should accept no substitutes. Pimm's No. 1 is said to have medicinal value. That's hardly surprising, since it tastes like cough syrup.

Ingredients
2 ounces Pimm's No. 1
5 to 7 ounces ginger ale, lemon-lime soda,
    or club soda
Cucumber slice

Preparation
Combine liquid ingredients in a highball glass filled with ice. Garnish with a cucumber slice.

PINK GIN

Strap on your pith helmet and enjoy this traditional drink of the British officer class, which, these days, is rarely served outside the United Kingdom and its former possessions. Also known as a Gin and Bitters, Pink Gin gets its astringent kick from Angostura Bitters, a tonic first developed by Johann Gottlieb Benjamin Siegert, a surgeon serving in Simón Bolivar's revolutionary army in South America, who sought to quell a rising tide of nausea among the soldiers in his care. Although it's highly doubtful this concoction will cure your stomach ailments, it will make you forget about them for a while. And then, perhaps, remember them all over again.

Ingredients
2 ounces gin
Dash Angostura bitters

Preparation
Stir ingredients with ice and strain into a cocktail glass.

"Lately I feel like my whole life has been a waste. I think I was meant to do something completely different."

—Ralph, 72, retired doorman

PISCO SOUR

No self-respecting old man should be afraid to drink a drink made with raw egg white. I mean, let's face it, how long have you got left anyway? So don't buy any green bananas and dare to try this frothy variation on the Whiskey Sour, which ups the ante via a tenfold increase in the risk that you might contract salmonella by drinking it. As an added bonus, it's also the national drink of Peru—although it was actually created by an American bartender working in Lima sometime before 1921. For best results, use authentic Pisco, a traditional Peruvian brandy developed by Spanish colonial settlers in the sixteenth century.

Ingredients
1½ ounces Pisco brandy
½ ounce fresh lemon juice
½ ounce simple syrup (see recipe on page 65)
1 whole egg white

Preparation
Combine all ingredients and shake vigorously with ice to froth up the egg white. Strain into a cocktail glass.

"A little booze'll make you charming.
A little more will make you an ass.
I hope to ride that line tonight."

—John, 68, painter

PLANTER'S PUNCH

Rum punches have been slaking the thirst of revelers at outdoor gatherings for centuries. Planter's Punch, a traditional welcoming drink served throughout the Caribbean, is one of the most popular. What old man wouldn't want to cool down with a ladleful of this on a hot summer's day? There's even a rhyming ditty—first printed in a 1908 edition of the *New York Times*—to help the mnemonically challenged keep the recipe straight.

> *This recipe I give to thee,*
> *Dear brother in the heat.*
> *Take two of sour (lime let it be)*
> *To one and a half of sweet,*
> *Of Old Jamaica pour three strong,*
> *And add four parts of weak.*
> *Then mix and drink. I do no wrong—*
> *I know whereof I speak.*

Ingredients

2 ounces dark rum
2 ounces orange juice
2 ounces pineapple juice
½ ounce lime juice
Dash grenadine
Maraschino cherry

Preparation

Combine the first four ingredients with ice and shake well. Strain into an ice-filled Collins glass. Top with grenadine. Garnish with a Maraschino cherry.

"I'm gonna die someday, so I may as well drink."

—Dick, 80, factory worker

"Things were better back then. You could trust your politicians, your newsmen, your actors. None of this *American Idol* shit."

—Louis, 73, pizza shop owner

PROHIBITION COCKTAIL

Prohibition was the best thing that ever happened to the cocktail industry. Nothing fosters innovation like the heavy hand of the government making things illegal. Like all drinks developed during that golden age of the American cocktail, this one relies on assertively flavored ingredients, which were used to disguise the harsh taste of the bathtub gin that would have been served in your typical speakeasy. So head over to your local juice joint, give your password to the big six at the door, pull up a stool next to your fellow swells, and watch the floor show. You'll be ossified in no time.

Ingredients
2 ounces gin
2 ounces white wine
1 teaspoon orange juice
½ teaspoon apricot brandy
Mint leaves

Preparation
Combine liquid ingredients with crushed ice in a cocktail glass. Garnish with mint leaves.

RACQUET CLUB COCKTAIL

Nothing caps off a vigorous round of Sunday morning squash with nieces and nephews quite like this variation of the martini, named after the New York City venue where it was first served. Loser buys the round, naturally, but since it's all coming out of the trust fund anyway, that's little consolation . . .

Ingredients
2 ounces gin
1 ounce dry vermouth
Dash orange bitters

Preparation
Shake all ingredients with ice and strain into a cocktail glass.

"Maybe our parents
weren't as stupid
as we thought
they were."

—John, 65, fisherman

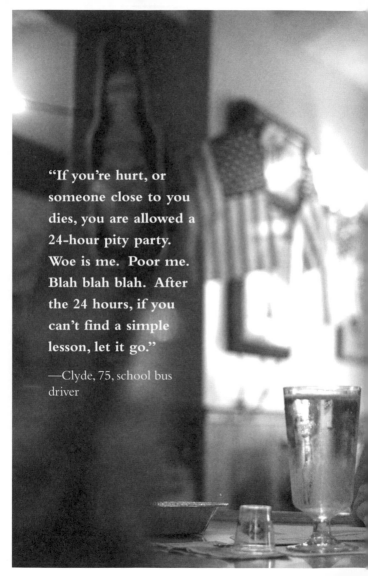

"If you're hurt, or someone close to you dies, you are allowed a 24-hour pity party. Woe is me. Poor me. Blah blah blah. After the 24 hours, if you can't find a simple lesson, let it go."

—Clyde, 75, school bus driver

ROB ROY

Of all the drinks named after nineteenth-century comic operas, the Rob Roy stands unchallenged. This mustiest of Old Man Drinks derives its name from a Scottish folk hero—kind of a poor man's Robin Hood—by way of an 1894 operetta about him by American composer Reginald De Koven, kind of a poor man's Gilbert and Sullivan. As every *really* old man knows, it was common practice at that time to name drinks after the new shows opening on Broadway (a round of Floradoras, anyone?). Hence the Rob Roy, a wan variation of the Manhattan that has lived on long after the musical that inspired it completely vanished from public consciousness.

Ingredients
2 ounces Scotch
1 ounce sweet vermouth
Dash orange bitters
Maraschino cherry

Preparation
Stir and strain liquid ingredients into a chilled cocktail glass. Garnish with a Maraschino cherry.

ROLLS-ROYCE

If you're in a bar drinking with old men at two in the morning, chances are you didn't arrive in a Rolls-Royce. But if you close your eyes and hammer back enough of these, you'll believe you did. Like the car for which it's named, it exudes the kind of Old World elegance every elderly barfly should possess, but few ever do.

Ingredients
1½ ounces gin
½ ounce dry vermouth
½ ounce sweet vermouth
1 teaspoon Benedictine

Preparation
Combine ingredients. Stir well with ice and then strain into a cocktail glass.

"Every town had a town drunk. But they weren't these smelly skid-row types you get now. Then, they were someone everyone knew. They were tolerated because we knew them and they were ours. Some of 'em we even grew up with. How's that?!"

—Don, 70, retired baseball coach

RUSTY NAIL

Never was a drink more aptly named. Forget what you may have heard about Drambuie's "honeyed sweetness." Sipping this is like taking a blow from the business end of a hammer. Drambuie, by the way, is a Gaelic word meaning "the drink that pleases." It pleases, all right. You know how they say that some drinks will put hair on your chest? This one could give you tetanus. Scottish bartenders used to stir it with an actual rusty nail, the better to sicken their obnoxious American customers. You'd best stick with a plastic stirrer and let the alcohol do the sickening.

Ingredients
2 ounces Scotch
1 ounce Drambuie

Preparation
Fill an old-fashioned glass with ice cubes. Pour in the Scotch and then gently add the Drambuie.

"You know, without my wife, I'd probably be living in an alleyway somewhere."

—Phil, 72, salesman

"My wife told me I should go out because it was nice out today. I said, 'Why? I'm 84 years old. By now I know what a nice day looks like.'"

—Richie, 84, retired limo driver

SALTY DOG

What self-respecting old man doesn't keep a carton of grapefruit juice in his refrigerator? This refreshing drink, made with simple ingredients that everyone has on hand, is a great alternative to the screwdriver, especially in warmer climes. It may have originated in Texas. In fact, a July 1947 edition of the *Brownsville Herald* sings the praises of the Salty Dog for its replenishing power, claiming that it "replaces salt sweated out in torrid Texas summers." Think of it as Gatorade with benefits. If salting the rim is too much trouble, skip that step and you've got yourself a Greyhound.

Ingredients
Salt
2 ounces vodka
3 ounces grapefruit juice

Preparation
Salt the rim of a highball glass filled with ice. Combine ingredients, shake well with ice, and pour into the highball glass.

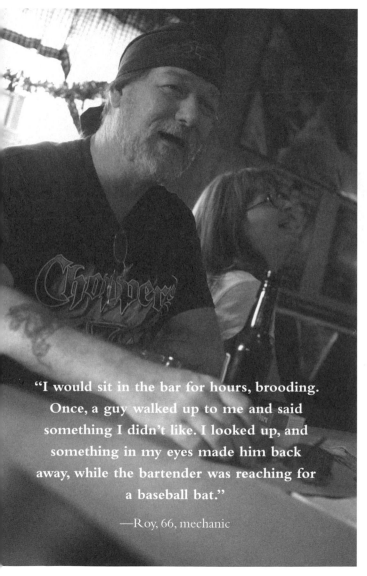

"I would sit in the bar for hours, brooding. Once, a guy walked up to me and said something I didn't like. I looked up, and something in my eyes made him back away, while the bartender was reaching for a baseball bat."

—Roy, 66, mechanic

"I've taken an involuntary vow of celibacy."

—Pablo, 69, janitor

SATAN'S WHISKERS

Satan's Whiskers has become something of a novelty cocktail, served at Halloween parties alongside the Zombie and the Bloody Mary, but this delicious orange-hued drink actually has a long and respectable pedigree dating back to the 1930s. Still, it's the diabolical name that usually hooks people. The drink has two variations: straight and curled. (It depends, one would assume, on whether the devil felt like applying his moustache wax that morning.) The curled version substitutes orange curaçao for the Grand Marnier. Try them both at the next meeting of the local Warlock Lodge.

Ingredients
¾ ounce gin
¾ ounce dry vermouth
¾ ounce sweet vermouth
½ ounce orange juice
½ ounce Grand Marnier
Dash orange bitters

Preparation
Shake all ingredients with ice and strain into a cocktail glass.

SAZERAC

Why does New Orleans produce so many great Old Man Drinks? There's the Grasshopper, the Hurricane, and this delightful concoction, which dates back to before the Civil War and is said by some to be the quintessential Big Easy cocktail. In 2008, the Louisiana state legislature seemed to recognize this fact when it proclaimed the Sazerac the "Official Cocktail of the City of New Orleans." And now that absinthe is legal again in the United States, you can take added satisfaction in preparing one according to the original recipe first devised by Creole apothecary Antoine Peychaud himself.

Ingredients
½ teaspoon absinthe
1 dash Peychaud's bitters
½ teaspoon simple syrup (see recipe on page 65)
2 ounces rye
Lemon twist

Preparation
Coat the bottom of a chilled Old Fashioned glass with absinthe. Add the bitters and simple syrup and then the rye. Garnish with a lemon twist.

"Hard drinking was just a fact of life. In some circles, it made you okay in their book."

—Walt, 72, musician

"Scotch goes well with anything,
especially marriage."

—Gary, 65, retired marketing manager

SCOTCH AND SODA

Here's one you can write the recipe for on the back of your hand. On second thought, bugger the recipe. It's Scotch . . . and soda. What part of Scotch and soda don't you understand? For a Scotch and water, substitute water for the soda. See how easy it is? This is a good one to make at the end of a long evening of drinking because there's really very little even a very intoxicated person could do to screw it up.

Ingredients
2 ounces Scotch
3 ounces club soda
Lime twist

Preparation
Pour Scotch into an Old Fashioned glass with a bit of ice. Fill the glass halfway with club soda and stir gently. Garnish with a lime twist.

SIDECAR

Veterans of the Great War will remember this one, first whipped up by the bartender at Harry's New York Bar in Paris to satisfy a U.S. Army captain who used a motorcycle sidecar as his principal means of transportation. After a few of these, you'd storm a trench for General Pershing, too.

Ingredients
½ ounce cognac
1 ounce Cointreau
¾ ounce fresh lemon juice
Lemon twist

Preparation
Sugar the rim of a cocktail glass. Shake liquid ingredients well with ice and then strain into a cocktail glass. Garnish with a twist of lemon.

"Most of us are afraid. When your fear comes to an end, then you discover the whole universe."

—Ceasar, 60, engineer and painter

SINGAPORE SLING

━━━━━━━━

When Humphrey Bogart wanted to drown his sorrows in *Casablanca*, he ordered one of these. When Somerset Maugham was looking for inspiration during his sojourn in Malaya, he knocked back a few of these. Yes, whenever world-weary men in warm-weather climates seek solace in the bottom of a Collins glass, the Singapore Sling is their drink of choice. Formerly known as the "Raffles Gin Sling," it was invented in 1915 by the delightfully named Ngiam Tong Boon, the bartender at the Raffles Hotel in Singapore, and quickly developed a loyal following. In the 1946 edition of *The Gentleman's Companion*, celebrated epicure Charles H. Baker Jr. called the Sling "an immortal, never-forgotten, delicious, slow-acting, insidious thing." Sounds like the kind of epitaph any right-thinking old man drinker would want for himself.

Ingredients

2 ounces gin
½ ounce Benedictine
½ ounce dry cherry brandy
Juice of half a lemon
2 dashes Angostura bitters

2 dashes orange bitters
Club soda
Lime twisl

Preparation
Combine the first six ingredients and shake well.
Strain into an ice-filled Collins glass. Top with club
soda. Garnish with a lime twist.

"Women! Turn 'em upside down, and they all look alike!"

—Michael, 71, baker

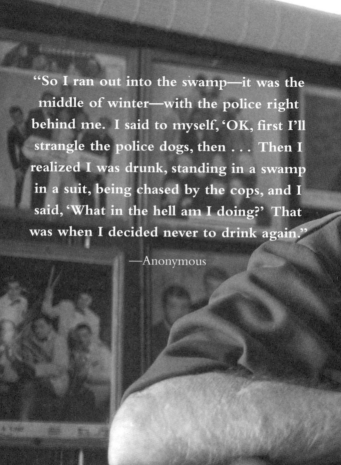

"So I ran out into the swamp—it was the middle of winter—with the police right behind me. I said to myself, 'OK, first I'll strangle the police dogs, then . . . Then I realized I was drunk, standing in a swamp in a suit, being chased by the cops, and I said, 'What in the hell am I doing?' That was when I decided never to drink again."

—Anonymous

SLOE GIN FIZZ

A fizz drink whose principal ingredient hasn't been widely available since World War II? *And* it contains egg white? You can't get more Old Man than that. The Sloe Gin Fizz takes you back to the days when men wore fur coats to college football games and sang "Boola Boola" at halftime. Club soda supplies the eponymous fizz, while sloe gin is a bittersweet gin-based liqueur flavored with sloe berries, the purplish fruit of a wild shrub native to England. Sadly, sloe gin is all but extinct these days—as is nearly everyone who ever drank it—but you can still find it gathering cobwebs on the back shelves of well-stocked liquor stores. Ask your bartender to prepare one of these and see what kind of look you get.

Ingredients

1½ ounces sloe gin
½ ounce dry gin
¾ ounce lemon juice
1 egg white
1 teaspoon sugar
Club soda

Preparation

Combine first five ingredients and shake vigorously
with ice. Strain into a highball glass filled with ice.
Top with club soda.

"I can just look at you and tell
I can please a woman better
than you. Although I am afraid
of spiders."

—Jeff, 69, ex-NYPD detective

STINGER

The plot of the 1948 film-noir classic *The Big Clock* turns on a handkerchief stained green with crème de menthe from this refreshingly sweet, minty cocktail. (Technically, the addition of green crème de menthe made that a Green Hornet, not a Stinger, but we'll overlook that to make the larger point that people last drank these during the Truman administration.) Typically served as a digestif, the Stinger dates back to the late nineteenth century (when it was originally called "The Judge"). It really became popular during Prohibition, when furtive tipplers turned to assertive flavors like mint to mask the harsh taste of bootleg spirits.

Ingredients
2 ounces cognac
1 ounce white crème de menthe

Preparation
Shake ingredients together and strain into a snifter filled with crushed ice.

"Where in the Constitution does it say that I can't get laid with whoever I want?"

—Juan, 67, retired construction worker

"I taught Bob Dylan how to do the butterfly stroke."

—Arvad, 65, filmmaker

TEQUILA SUNRISE

"A Fascinating Tequila Fantasy" screamed the brochure at the Agua Caliente racetrack in Mexico, where this cocktail was born. Intended as a hangover cure for horseplayers who had overindulged the night before, the Sunrise takes its name from its glowing orange hue once all the ingredients have settled in the glass. It dates back to the 1920s, although it didn't really catch on stateside until the 1970s, when a hit song by the Eagles and a resurgence of interest in tequila put it back on the brunch menu. Stiffen your spine for a long day playing the ponies with one of these the next time business or pleasure takes you to Hialeah.

Ingredients
2 ounces tequila
4 ounces orange juice
1 ounce grenadine
Lime wedge

Preparation
Pour the tequila into a highball glass filled with ice and then add the orange juice. Slowly add the grenadine and stir. Garnish with a lime wedge.

TOM AND JERRY

Once upon a time, this drink was as ubiquitous as egg nog on Christmas Eve. (Damon Runyon once wrote that it was "so popular that many people think Christmas is invented only to furnish an excuse for a hot Tom and Jerry.") Then the spirit of Scrooge took over, and people became unduly squeamish about putting raw eggs in their cocktails. Overnight, it seemed, the T&J went the way of the holiday fruitcake, never to be spoken of again. Put a little old school back in your yuletide celebration by reviving this drink, which was first concocted by British sportswriter Pierce Egan and named after two characters from his 1821 novel *Life in London*.

Ingredients

1 teaspoon sugar
1 whole egg yolk
1 ounce dark rum
1 whole egg white
Boiling water
Dash brandy
Nutmeg

Preparation

Beat the sugar into the egg yolk, add the rum, and incorporate the egg white. Transfer into a coffee mug and fill with boiling water. Add the brandy and garnish with grated nutmeg.

"I was a Marine. We were a hard-drinking lot. On port call, we'd go and terrorize all of the bars, especially the ones with Army or Navy there. We'd tear the place up, have a good brawl, apologize and make friends, and then everyone would get drunk. Drunker."

—Max, 66, salesman

TOM COLLINS

This is another one of those old, old drinks with a murky pedigree that even cocktail historians have a hard time keeping straight. If you were alive in 1874 and someone asked if you'd seen Tom Collins, then you were about to become the victim of a strange and Byzantine practical joke—the *Punk'd* of its day—known as the Great Tom Collins Hoax. That *may* have inspired the name of this cocktail, which just as plausibly could have come from a mashup of John Collins—a London head-waiter who had a popular gin punch named after him—and Old Tom, the brand of sweet gin originally used to make this drink. Who really knows for sure? All we do know is the Tom Collins was all the rage in the 1870s and should be consumed, in the words of noted epicure David Embury, author of *The Fine Art of Mixing Drinks*, "slowly, with reverence and meditation."

Ingredients
2 ounces gin
1 ounce lemon juice
1 teaspoon superfine sugar
3 ounces club soda
Maraschino cherry

Preparation

Combine the first three ingredients with ice and shake. Strain into a Collins glass half-filled with ice cubes. Add the club soda and stir. Garnish with a Maraschino cherry.

"I never had a threesome, but it's bound to happen soon."

—Fred, 90, retired janitor

"I still go to my local watering hole, once in a while, but it ain't the same anymore. Different crowd, all of the old-timers are mostly gone. I'm a dinosaur, huh?"

—Patrick, 65, trucker

VIEUX CARRÉ

The Vieux Carré is another Big Easy classic, and is named after the city's famed French Quarter. Invented in 1938 by Walter Bergeron, the head bartender at the Monteleone Hotel, the Vieux Carré was on the Endangered Cocktail List until a 1990s revival. The rather complicated ingredients list reflects the demographic composition of the Quarter at the time: American (rye whiskey), Italian (vermouth), and French (cognac).

Ingredients
¾ ounce rye
¾ ounce sweet vermouth
¾ ounce cognac
⅛ ounce Benedictine
2 dashes Angostura bitters
2 dashes Peychaud's bitters
Lemon peel

Preparation
Mix all liquid ingredients in a rocks glass with ice. Garnish with lemon peel.

WARD EIGHT

Ward Eight sounds like the wing of a nursing home or a drunk tank—the kind of place to which no self-respecting old man wants to be consigned before his time. But in fact this drink gets its name from a political subdivision—Boston's eighth ward, to be precise—where, in 1898, the bartender at the Locke-Ober Café created this drink to commemorate the victory of crooked political boss Martin Lomasney, the so-called Czar of Ward Eight, in his race for the state legislature. There was just one problem: Lomasney was an avowed teetotaler. (As a matter of fact, his drink of choice was tea.) That left a few extra Ward Eights to dole out on Election Day, when voters were also plied with premarked ballots to ensure the proper outcome. Exercise your own franchise by voting for this tart, tasty Beantown favorite.

Ingredients

1½ ounces bourbon
½ ounce lemon juice
½ ounce orange juice
1 teaspoon grenadine

Preparation

Shake all ingredients with ice. Strain into a cocktail glass.

"None of these foo-foo beers.
We drank Schlitz and Narragansett. You
know Narragansett? They used to advertise
'made from the cool, clear waters of
Narragansett Bay.' Well, Narragansett Bay
was, and is, a scumhole. You could float a
piece of steel on it. 'S OK, we still drank
the shit."

—Leo, 88, retired military

WHISKEY SOUR

The Whiskey Sour dates back to at least 1870 but came into fashion in the 1960s, when sour mix was first mass-marketed as the Holy Grail of every well-stocked home bar. ("Most people can't make a Whiskey Sour as good as this, and I wish they wouldn't try," macho actor Jack Palance boasted in a famous print ad for Heublein brand sour mix, circa 1967.) The truly dedicated old man eschews sour mix altogether, of course, and squeezes the lemons for this drink himself. Throw in an egg white and you've got yourself a Boston Sour.

Ingredients
1 ounce lemon juice
1 teaspoon powdered sugar
2 ounces blended Scotch whiskey
Lemon slice
Maraschino cherry

Preparation
Shake all liquid ingredients together and strain into a sour glass. Garnish with a slice of lemon and a cherry.

"There are times you drink 'til you fall on your face. Then there are times when you drink and someone else falls on your face. Here's hoping I have more of those times."

— Dennis, 67, musician

SELECTED BIBLIOGRAPHY

In addition to seeking out the wisdom of professional and amateur mixologists worldwide, I consulted the following books in compiling the drink recipes included in this volume:

Broom, Dave. *New American Bartender's Handbook*. San Diego, CA: Thunder Bay Press, 2003.

Chirico, Rob. *Field Guide to Cocktails*. Philadelphia, PA: Quirk Books, 2005.

Craddock, Harry. *The Savoy Cocktail Book*. New York: Richard R. Smith, 1930.

Cotton, Leo. *Old Mr. Boston Deluxe Official Bartender's Guide*. Boston, MA: Mr. Boston Distiller, Inc., 1960.

Duffy, Patrick Gavin. *The Standard Bartender's Guide*. Garden City, NY: Permabooks, 1948.

Embury, David A. *The Fine Art of Mixing Drinks*. New York: Mud Puddle Books, 2008.

Felten Eric. *How's Your Drink? Cocktails, Culture, and the Art of Drinking Well*. Evanston, IL: Agate Publishing, 2007.

Grimes, William. *Straight Up or On the Rocks: The Story of the American Cocktail*. New York: North Point Press, 2001.

Kingwell, Mark. *Classic Cocktails: A Modern Shake*. New York: St. Martin's Press, 2007.

Regan, Gary. *The Joy of Mixology*. New York: Clarkson Potter, 2003.

Sennett, Bob, ed. *Complete World Bartender Guide*. New York: Bantam Books, 1981.

ACKNOWLEDGMENTS

This book would not have been possible without the hard work of the following field researchers, who braved inebriation and its aftereffects to provide many of the great quotations featured herein: Paul Slimak, Christina Berner, Samantha Rosenberg, Christopher M. Arthur, Kate Addicott, Jon Protas, and Jesse Bernardini.

ABOUT THE AUTHOR

Robert Schnakenberg is the author of several nonfiction books, including *Secret Lives of Great Authors*, *The Encyclopedia Shatnerica*, and *Distory: A Treasury of Historical Insults*. His favorite Old Man Drinks include the Gimlet, the Cuba Libre, and the Gin and Tonic.